Joanna Sheen's World of Cards

Dedication
To all my family and friends,
who encourage me with my cards
and surround me with love.

Joanna Sheen's
World of Cards

SEARCH PRESS

First published in paperback in Great Britain 2010

Search Press Limited
Wellwood, North Farm Road,
Tunbridge Wells, Kent TN2 3DR

First published in hardback in Great Britain 2009

ISBN: 978-1-84448-600-7

Publisher's note
All the step-by-step photographs in this book feature the author, Joanna Sheen, demonstrating how to make greetings cards. No models have been used.

You are invited to visit the author's website at:
www.joannasheen.com

If you have any queries about any aspect of making the cards, or what specific materials were used, please feel free to email me at Joanna@joannasheen.com and my team and I will do our best to help you.

Printed in Malaysia

Acknowledgements

This was a giant project and I am so grateful to everyone that helped. I simply could not have managed it alone!

Thank you Edd Ralph from Search Press for being a great editor – it has been so easy working with you – and to Roz Dace, also from Search Press, for keeping an eye on us!
Thank you Debbie Patterson for such pretty photos; it is always so good working with you.

The other stars of the book are the team of cardmakers that helped by making some of the cards that feature in this book – thank you from the bottom of my heart to:
Tina Dorr, Pamela Manning, Eunice Meeus, Suzanne Saltwell, Elaine Smith, Sue Thorpe and Jo Westwick.

Search Press is delighted to announce that

Joanna Sheen's World of Cards

has been declared the 2009 Craft Awards **'Best Craft Book'**, as voted for by the readers of *Crafts Beautiful, Let's Make Cards!* and *Let's Get Crafting!* magazines.

Visit www.craftawards.com for more details.

Contents

Introduction 6

Basic materials 8

Lady's birthday 10
Pretty Periwinkles

Man's birthday 16
Pharaoh's View

Child's birthday 22
The Star Tiger

21st birthday 28
Key to the Door

Mothering Sunday 34
Spring Spirit

Father's Day 40
Wild West

St Valentine's Day 46
Clearly Yours

Wedding 50
Only a Rose

Anniversary 58
High Spirits

Thank you 64
Leopard Song

Congratulations 68
Life at Sea

Christening 72
Infant Treasures

Christmas 78
Holy Night

Christmas 86
Santa Box

With sympathy 94
Remembered

Missing you 100
Kitten Curl

Belated 106
Butterflies

Retirement 110
Clover Field

New home 116
Moving Day

New job 122
Dive Right In

Index 128

Introduction

Welcome to my world of cards. Cards, flowers and crafting have been lifetime passions for me. We have been running our craft company for thirty years now so I make no apologies for believing that creating things makes an important contribution to the world. Handmade items show that you care and that you have given the most precious of all gifts: your time.

Some of the cards in this book are simple and great for beginners. Once you are happy with these, try some of the more complex cards, and if you fancy the rewards of making more challenging cards, there are some really stunning examples for you to make. There are also lots of ideas to fill you with inspiration!

I hope you will enjoy exploring the book and pausing to look at the pretty photographs. I hope you will also find many of the hints, tips and recipes come in handy when you get stuck for inspiration. Happy cardmaking!

Recipes

Throughout the book I have added some useful hints and tips, some of my favourite quotations and sayings, and many of my family's recipes that we have used at so many gatherings and celebrations!

You can find them in boxes like this one.

Tools and equipment

All the way through the book you'll find little notes, like this one, on the tools and equipment used in a project. They can help you by adding an extra hint or tip on how to use the tool or piece of equipment to make cards.

Basic materials

Pictured here are all the basic tools and equipment that you will see me using over and over again in the book. Obviously there are hundreds more bits and pieces you might want to collect as you progress with cardmaking, but these tools I really can not be without!

Double-sided sticky tape – This has to be one of my greatest helpers in making cards! I use this tape in roller dispensers too.

2mm (1/32in) foam tape – This is so useful for adding a bit of extra dimension to a card and supporting parts of cards.

Single-sided sticky tape – There are lots of instances when you might want to tack something down with single-sided tape rather than double-sided.

Small sharp scissors – These are specialist decoupage snips and invaluable for cutting out small details.

General scissors – There are many different brands out there but go for some that are both comfortable and suitably sharp.

Large scissors – When you are cutting an entire page, or large areas in general, these will be just what you need.

Tweezers – I am rarely seen without tweezers sitting right beside me. Well worth taking the time to get the hang of them, they really are my favourite tool.

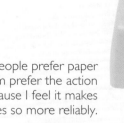

Guillotine – Some people prefer paper trimmers, but I am prefer the action of a guillotine because I feel it makes straighter cuts and does so more reliably.

Cutting mat – Always protect any surface you are using by having a good craft mat that will take bumps, knocks and paint spills!

Large soft brush – This style of soft brush is easily available in craft shops and is excellent for removing small bits from the surface or a card and general cleaning.

Embellishments

Ribbon – A particular passion of mine – particularly organza which is light, floaty and very forgiving!

Outline stickers or **peel-offs** – Another must-have that make design much easier, these allow you to use words, numbers, corners or straight lines to emphasise particular areas.

Decorative brads – There must be a million different styles out there, so collect some favourites!

Stickers – These are often used in cardmaking and again, many different designs are available.

Tassels – I have a passion for tassels (yet another one!) and like to use them whenever it is appropriate on a card.

Craft jewels – Diamante, rhinestones, call them what you will, these adhesive fake jewels always add some extra pizzazz to a card!

Metallic felt-tip pens – I use these wide-nibbed calligraphy pens all the time. I think they are brilliant.

HB pencil – A good standard pencil is essential for marking and drawing round objects.

White pencil – This is invaluable if you are working with black or dark card.

Other useful tools

Other things I use on occasion include the following.

Eraser – Handy for tidying away any pencil markings.

Steel-edged ruler – This is mainly used for measuring, but it is also used for cutting against, and occasionally tearing.

Craft knife – I sometimes use these in conjunction with scissors to get to the tiniest parts of decoupage.

Embossing stylus – This can be used on brass stencils and also on scoring boards.

Waterbrush – This paintbrush holds a reservoir of water, but you could use a regular watercolour brush.

Cotton buds – Just the thing for cleaning up tiny bits of ink on stamps and for other small cleaning jobs.

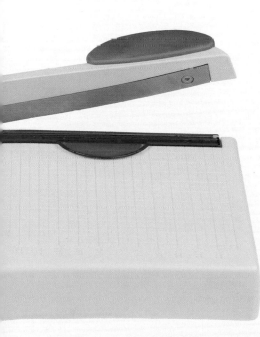

Lady's birthday
Pretty Periwinkles

This very feminine card combines periwinkle pictures with real pressed flowers to make something very special for a birthday. If you want to make the card less complicated, you can skip the pressed flowers, but once you have mastered their use, it would be a shame to leave such pretty things out. Tweezers come into play here as they are by far the most efficient way of handling pressed flowers without breaking them.

Remember that this card, in common with all the others in the book, is here to give you ideas and inspiration as well as for you to copy. If you do not have this exact flower picture then use another design featuring something botanical instead.

Materials

One 21 x 15cm (8¼ x 6in)
sheet of lilac card
One 21 x 15cm (8¼ x 6in) sheet of
heavyweight acetate
One 30 x 21cm (12 x 8¼in) sheet of
card printed with backing design
Periwinkle pictures
Selection of pale blue and lilac pressed
flowers and leaves
Lilac and blue organza ribbon
Tweezers
Double-sided tape
Scissors
Bone folder and scoring board
Silicone glue and cocktail stick
Japanese screw punch
Cutting mat

*Birthdays are good for you.
The more you have, the
longer you live.*

Anonymous

The bone folder and
scoring board

You can make your card blanks by just folding and sharpening the crease with a bone folder or you can use one of the many scoreboards on the market to make a really accurate crease that helps you fold perfectly.

Design CDs

Design CDs can be like a store cupboard of images for you – always available when you need something. This set features the artwork of the artist Jayne Netley Mayhew – she is a truly wonderful watercolour painter and there are animal and floral designs aplenty to inspire and help you create your own greetings card masterpiece!

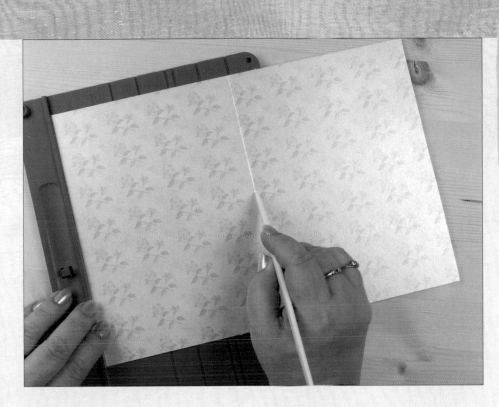

Tip

If your printer does not accept card, you can simply mount the backing paper on to a piece of plain card.

1 Score down the centre of the card printed with the backing paper design and fold it in half.

2 Cut out the largest periwinkle picture and mount it on to a 10.5cm × 14cm (4⅛ × 5½in) piece of lilac card, using double-sided tape. Attach both to the main card, placing them on the top left and securing them with double-sided tape.

3 Arrange the pressed leaves on the card, and once you are happy with the shape of the spray, secure the leaves in place with tiny amounts of silicone glue applied with a cocktail stick.

5 Once the glue is dry, open up the card and place it flat on a cutting mat. Place the sheet of acetate over the front, and use the Japanese screw punch to make two holes near the spine as shown.

4 Attach the other pieces of foliage and flowers, again securing them with tiny amounts of silicone glue.

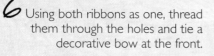

Tip

Holding the ends of the two ribbons with the tweezers makes it much easier to feed them through the holes.

6 Using both ribbons as one, thread them through the holes and tie a decorative bow at the front.

Preserving Roses

If you want to keep some roses from a special bouquet, take each stem and strip it of most of its leaves. Next, bundle five or so roses together using an elastic band and use a coat hanger to suspend them in a warm, airy spot such as a wardrobe or airing upboard.

The elastic band clings around the stems and contracts as they shrink, which is important: if you use string they will all drop on the floor!

You can tell if they are dry by pressing your thumbnail into the calyx just under the flower; if it is hard then they are ready. It usually takes from three weeks to a month for them to dry completely.

You can either make a little arrangement with them or just keep them tied with a pretty ribbon in a memory box.

Pretty Periwinkles

A lovely, harmonious collection of blues and lilacs create a really restful,
serene feel to this feminine card.

Bougainvillea Bookmark

These sprays of bougainvillea contrast beautifully with the dark background and a matching bookmark is attached at the bottom of the card.

Fabulous Fans

A clear acetate card makes a wonderful change and is sure to be admired; here some embossed parchment fans have been used as a centrepiece – the basics on using an acetate card are on pages 47–48.

Lilac Butterflies

Pretty lilacs and purple are used together here, along with some die-cut shapes and embossing.

Tip

Any of these cards would be wonderful ideas for a feminine birthday token. You could make a card almost identical to one from the picture or just use it as inspiration!

1920s Beauty

This lovely card has a waterfall technique incorporated on to the front (see pages 51–55 for the technique). The sepia photograph could be anyone from your family collection or you can source it from elsewhere.

Wild Roses

These wild roses are stamped and coloured and pretty pink ribbon provides the frame for them.

Vintage Fans

The fan is stamped and embossed with sparkly white powder on parchment. Again, you could use a family photograph or a bought one.

Pharaoh's View

The pyramage technique complements the theme of the card extremely well.

Your birthday is a special time to celebrate the gift of 'you' to the world.

Anonymous

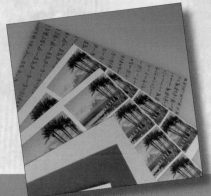

Man's birthday

Pharaoh's View

Great for the man in your life

Some people feel it is sometimes a little harder to come up with a perfect card for a male relative or friend, but I enjoy the challenge and for this birthday card I have used some Egyptian artwork that makes it perfect for someone keen on travel or history.

This card uses a technique that is referred to as pyramage, where the pictures start out at the same size and each subsequent layer is trimmed slightly smaller all the way round. This gives a stepped effect to the design once the pieces are layered.

Materials

One 30 x 21cm (12 x 8¼in) sheet of antique gold card

Two 30 x 21cm (12 x 8¼in) sheets of off-white pearl card

One 30 x 21cm (12 x 8¼in) sheet of hieroglyphic backing card

Five identical Egyptian landscape pictures and three identical Tutankhamun pictures

Tweezers

Guillotine

Bone folder and scoring board

Scissors

Double-sided tape

2mm (1/32in) foam tape

1 Score a line down the centre of the off-white pearl card and fold, sharpening the crease with a bone folder. Cut the gold card down to sit on top of the pearl card, leaving a 5mm (¼in) border all round.

2 Secure the gold card in place with foam tape, then attach a piece of hieroglyphics backing paper in place with double-sided tape, trimming it down beforehand to leave a 5mm (¼in) border all round.

3 Put one of the Egyptian landscape pictures to one side, then trim 5mm (¼ in) from each side of the second.

4 Trim 10mm (¼ in) from each side of the third, 15mm (½ in) from each side of the fourth, and 20mm (¾ in) from each side of the fifth. It is important to take some from all of the sides, or you will not get the correct effect at the end. This will give you five images as shown.

5 Use double-sided tape to mount the largest image on off-white and then gold card, leaving 5mm (¼ in) borders each time.

6 Attach the mounted piece to the left-hand side of the card with double-sided tape, then mount the smaller landscape images on top. Place them centrally each time, and work from largest to smallest, using foam tape each time.

7 Take the pictures of Tutankhamun and cut away the background from the first. Cut the background and chest away from the second; and cut away everything but the face from the third.

8 Use silicone glue to secure the largest picture to the lower right of the card, then secure the smaller pieces in place in turn to finish the card (see right).

Vintage Map

This card uses vintage map artwork from a Victorian-themed source CD, but you could use an old map you have tinted with a sepia inkpad.

Young Lad

This decoupage card gets its attractive shape from using a corner punch to decorate all the corners.

Bulldog Pocket

This fun card, in the shape of a pocket, uses an old button as an embellishment and some tags with an amusing bulldog character on them.

Pioneer Campsite

A sandy background tones well with
the cowboy scene. This card uses the
pyramage technique featured in the
main project.

Bucking Bronco

This is a gatefold card (see pages 40–42 for the
technique) with the addition of a deliberately
skewed topper to reflect the bronco!

Tip

If you are making a
card for someone you
know well try and think
laterally: take their
hobby or interest and
use that as inspiration
– or perhaps think of an
unusual story connected
with that person.

Tip

I am reliably informed by my nephew that all proper boys' cards should have a badge attached as that's the best bit. These are easily bought and if it is going to make them smile that is fine by me!

The Star Tiger

This is a stunning card that looks far harder to make than it really is – have a go and amaze someone with your skill!

Tip

To make a card even more appealing to a child, how about storing the card in a box or bag with some cotton wool dotted with drops of some fruit- or chocolate-scented essential oil.

Child's birthday
The Star Tiger

Making a star card may seem intimidating as it is a little out of the ordinary, but once you have completed one you will see how relatively simple they are. They look lovely when they are finished.

Making cards for children can be such fun – just pick a theme you know they will enjoy and run with it: the bigger and bolder the better!

Materials

Two 30 x 21cm (12 x 8¼in)
sheets of grassy/neutral backing paper

Selection of domestic and
wild cat images

Three 20 x 10cm (8 x 4in)
pieces of pale beige card

Five 20 x 10cm (8 x 4in)
pieces of dark tan card

One 30 x 21cm (12 x 8¼in)
sheet of dark brown card

One 30 x 21cm (12 x 8¼in)
sheet of dark beige card

Length of 7mm (¼in) ribbon

Tweezers

Double-sided tape

Bone folder and scoring board

Die-cutter and cat design die-cut

Glue stick

Scissors

Die-cutter and die-cuts

There are many different die-cutting tools on the market at the moment – the cats in this project were made using this particular gadget – but cat dies are available on many other systems too!

1 Take the pieces of pale beige card and fold each one in half using the bone folder and scoring board. Do the same with three pieces of the tan card, making sure the coloured side is on the inside of all the pieces.

23

2 Take the two remaining pieces of the tan card and cut each in half to give you four 10 x 10cm (4 x 4in) squares of card. Put one to the side for another project, and cut one in half along the diagonal to make two triangles.

3 Take one of the folded pieces and place double-sided tape on one side as shown (see inset). Repeat on the other five pieces.

4 Begin to assemble the card by removing the backing from one of the beige pieces and pressing it on to the untaped side of one of the tan pieces.

5 Remove the backing from the tan piece, then attach the untaped side of a beige piece to it.

6 Repeat the process with the remaining three pieces, alternating the colours. When you reach the final piece, do not remove the tape.

The best birthdays are those that have not yet arrived!

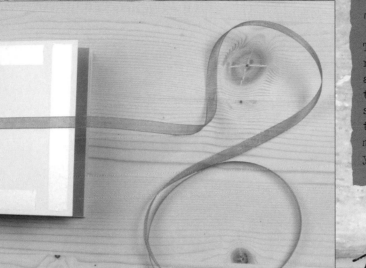

7 Remove the backing from the final piece and use the tape to secure a 45cm (17¾in) length of ribbon to the piece as shown.

8 Place one of the squares from step 2 on to the card, over the ribbon, and make the back cover of the card.

9 Turn the card over, run tape around all four sides, secure a 45cm (17¾in) ribbon, and place the final square on top to make the front cover. Next, run tape along the short sides of the triangle and secure this to the inside of the front cover. This makes a small pocket for a gift voucher.

10 Cut out thirteen different pictures from the sheets of cats, making sure that they are all similar sizes. If your pictures do not have a border, or are the wrong shape, mount them on 7.5 x 7.5cm (3 x 3in) squares of the grassy/neutral backing paper.

11 Use the die-cutter with the kitten die-cut to make two kittens, one in dark beige and one in dark brown. Mount the dark brown details on the dark beige base, and the dark beige details on the dark brown base, using the glue stick and tweezers to attach them (see inset). Use the glue stick to attach the die-cut kittens to the inside front cover.

12 Use double-sided tape to attach a cat picture on every inside page, and on the front cover.

13 You can tie the card closed with a bow (see inset), or use a bow to secure it open, like a star.

Teddy o'Clock

This fun teddy card has the look of a clock with the same teddy face being stamped repeatedly in different colours around the octagonal shape.

Mischievous Girls

Here the young ladies artwork has been decoupaged. The original is by a Victorian illustrator called Kate Greenaway.

Ballet Class

This gentle picture of a young ballerina is beautifully embellished with flowers and gems.

Headdress

This card is a standard gatefold with a cowboy picture inside and this fun headdress on the topper.

21st birthday
Key to the Door

This vintage lady and the perfume bottles are from a design CD but you could use this idea with a sepia photograph and pictures of bottles you have at home.

Gold leaf

The gold leaf used in this project comes in very thin sheets and is relatively inexpensive (it is extremely thin!). Although it needs handling with care it gives a pretty effect and is well worth experimenting with.

Devon Cream Truffles

50ml (2fl.oz, or 1¾ US fl.oz) double cream
50g (1¾oz) butter at room temperature
175g (6oz) good quality chocolate
25ml (1fl.oz, or ⅞ US fl.oz) your choice of alcohol
Drinking chocolate powder or nuts for decoration

Reduce the cream by boiling it in a heavy-based pan for a few minutes. Lower the heat, then break the chocolate into small pieces and place it in the cream. Add the alcohol and stir until the chocolate has melted, then add the butter.
  Once the mixture is smooth, pour it into a dish and leave it in the fridge until firm. Using a teaspoon, shape the mixture into balls and roll in either drinking chocolate powder or nuts. Keep them in the fridge until ten minutes before serving.

Materials

One 42 x 30cm (16½ x 12in) sheet of opal/ivory card
One 30 x 21cm (12 x 8¼in) sheet of coral card
Two 30 x 21cm (12 x 8¼in) sheets of gold card
One 21 x 15cm (8¼ x 6in) sheet of heavyweight acetate
One 30 x 21cm (12 x 8¼in) sheet of clear double-sided adhesive
Sheet of lady and selection of perfume bottle pictures
Rubber stamp: Blossom and swan fan
Peel-off stickers of the numbers 2 and 1
Sheet of gold leaf
Peach and lilac 7mm (¼in) ribbons
Tweezers
Archival black inkpad
Scissors
Double-sided tape
Sharp scissors
2mm (¹⁄₃₂in) foam tape
Silicone glue and cocktail stick

Key to the Door

A beautiful face, perfume, a fan and some lovely touches of gold leaf!

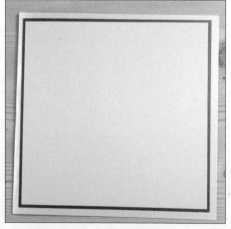

1 Make sure the acetate is clean, and use the archival ink to stamp a fan on to it. Once dry, use the scissors to cut roughly around it.

2 Remove one backing cover from the clear double-sided adhesive sheet and place the fan on to the sheet (see inset). Cut it out, peel off the remaining backing and place the gold leaf on to the sticky side. Gently pull away the excess gold leaf.

Success is not the Key to happiness. Happiness is the Key to success. If you love what you are doing, you will be successful.

Albert Schweitzer

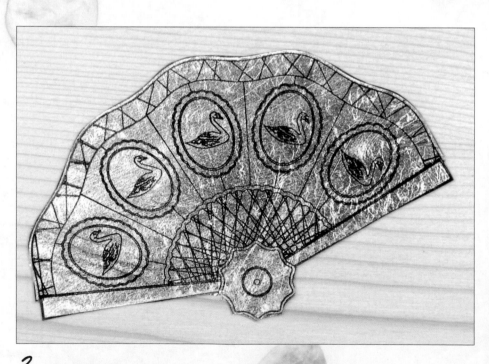

3 Turn the fan over and use sharp scissors to cut carefully round the outline of the fan.

4 Fold the opal/ivory piece of card in half, and then use the guillotine to cut it down to make a card 20.5cm (8in) square. Use 2mm (1/32in) foam tape to mount a 20cm (7¾in) square of the gold card on top of the opal/ivory card; and use double-sided tape to mount a 19.5cm (7½in) square of coral card on top of the gold piece.

5 Cut out the largest lady picture and use double-sided tape to mount it on a piece of gold card that is just large enough to leave a 5mm (1/8in) border all round it. Mount the piece on the main card using 2mm (1/32in) foam tape.

6 Cut out four large and two small perfume bottles. Curving each piece slightly, use quite large blobs of silicone glue to adhere the large bottles to the card, on the right-hand-side.

7 Use silicone glue to secure the fan below the picture, and then attach the small perfume bottles in the same way, overlapping the fan as shown.

8 Complete the card by using the stickers to put a '21' in the top left-hand corner, and then make a bow with the two ribbons. Use silicone glue to attach the bow to the fan.

31

Vintage Victoriana
This card has an acetate layer on the front with the Victorian gentleman underneath and a lady rendered in gold leaf on top of the acetate.

Old Gold
Using a combination of printing and stamped images, this card has a lovely junk jewellery brooch as an embellishment.

Exploding Lilacs
This exploding box is made in the same way as the one on pages 86–91. It makes a very pretty keepsake for the recipient.

Sophisticated Lady
The fun of making this card is colouring the bubbles with some glaze to make them really pop!

Purple Star
These lovely purple and lilac tones look gorgeous when seen alongside the silver embellishments used in this card.

Mothering Sunday
Spring Spirit

A beautiful floral envelope

Aspecial card for your mother is something she will always treasure, so planning something different is well worth the time.

This basic envelope shape is so versatile for greetings cards that once you have made one, I am sure you will think of dozens of other themes you can use to make more. It is a good standby that I often fall back on.

Materials

One 45 x 20cm (17¾ x 7¾in) double-fold card blank
One 30 x 21cm (12 x 8¼in) sheet of antique gold card
Botanical decoupage sheets
Gold line peel-offs
Two co-ordinating backing papers
Scissors
Tweezers
Silicone glue
Cocktail sticks
Guillotine

Silicone glue and cocktail sticks

Silicone glue and similar products are simply the best adhesive for decoupage and attaching embellishments to cards. I dispense the glue by squeezing a blob very gently on to a cocktail stick and placing in position. The cocktail stick can be thrown away after use to help keeps things clean and tidy!

I The card blank has three 15 x 20cm (6 x 7⅞in) panels with score lines between each. Use a guillotine to trim one of the outside panels to the same shape as an envelope as shown.

Tip

I cut the envelope shape by eye, but you might like to use an envelope as a template and mark the card blank with a pencil.

Tip

If the decoupage sheet you are using is of smaller flowers, you may need more pieces to cover the edge of the envelope.

2 Carefully cut out layers 1 and 2 from two decoupage sheets (see inset) and use a cocktail stick to smear silicone glue over the back of each piece before placing it on the flap.

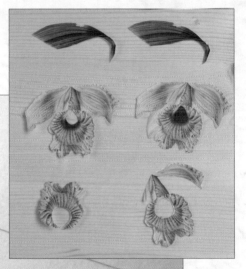

3 Cut out some additional details from the decoupage sheets (see inset). Slip some of the smaller pieces between the larger flowers, to make sure that the edge of the envelope effect is completely covered, then give each of the remaining ones a slight curve with your fingers before adding thicker blobs of silicone glue to layer it on to the flowers on the edge of the envelope.

Today is the tomorrow you worried about yesterday!

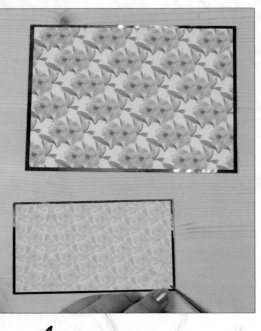

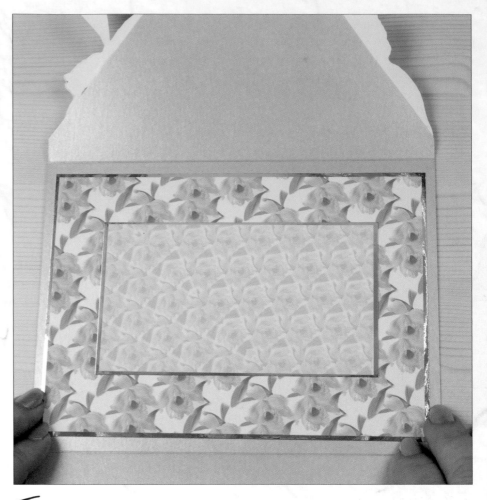

4 Cut two rectangles of gold card, one 19 x 13.5cm (7½ x 5¼in) and the other 14 x 8cm (5½ x 3⅛in). Cut a rectangle of the first backing paper so that it fits on top of the larger gold rectangle, leaving a 5mm (¼in) border all round. Attach it with double-sided tape, then make a second rectangle of the other backing paper that fits on the other gold rectangle, leaving a similar border. Stick these together with double-sided tape.

5 Turn the envelope card over, and use double-sided tape to attach the larger rectangle to the inside of the central panel. Layer the smaller rectangle on to the top of this, again securing it with double-sided tape.

6 Fold the third panel up, over the rectangles. Assemble a third decoupage flower as before, and attach it to the card with smeared silicone glue. Complete the decoration by attaching two gold line peel-off strips.

7 Close the envelope flap to finish.

Spring Spirit

The closed card looks just like a decorated envelope – the flap lifts to reveal a single flower and then opens to show the centre of the card where you can write your message.

You can keep cut flowers fresher for longer by adding one or two small pieces of charcoal to the vase of water.

Clockwise from top left:

Thoughtful Lady

The illustration used for the decoupage is by the Victorian artist Kate Greenaway and has been decoupaged and embellished with organza ribbon.

The Sewing Silhouette

This card is so dainty and feminine – the corners of the topper are achieved with a paper punch, and the picture comes from a design CD.

Butterfly Box

This exploding box (for instructions on this technique see pages 86–91) is a delightful way to show your mother how much you care. You could also make one using photographs instead of flowers to make it even more personal.

The butterflies inside and on top of the exploding box are printed out on inkjet acetate and they look so realistic!

Father's Day
Wild West

Although Father's Day has not been established as long as Mothering Sunday as far as celebrations are concerned, I think it is a very important way of saying 'thank you, Dad, for being you!'

This card shows how to make the basic gatefold shape that can be used in masses of different ways, so is a good fold to try out if it is new to you!

Materials

One 42 x 30cm (16½ x 12in) sheet of black card

One 30 x 21cm (12 x 8¼in) sheet of yellow card

One landscape picture from an American frontier-themed CD

One 30 x 21cm (12 x 8¼in) sheet of copper card

Scissors

Tweezers

Bone folder and scoring mat

Guillotine

Tip

Instead of buying a gift for your dad, how about suggesting something like a free car wash or offering to cook him his favourite meal or cake? Set it up as an IOU for him to claim when he would like to take you up on the offer!

1 Cut the black card down to 40 x 13.5cm (15¾ x 5¼in). Measure 10cm (4in) in from the short end and score down this line. Fold the side in, then repeat on the other short end to make a gatefold in the base card as shown.

2 Cut down the large landscape picture until it measures 15 x 8.5cm (6 x 3¼in), then carefully cut it exactly in half using the guillotine.

3 Cut a 15.5 × 9cm (6 × 3½in) rectangle of copper card; a 16 × 9.5cm (6¼ × 3¾in) rectangle of yellow card; and a 16.5 × 10cm (6½ × 4in) rectangle of copper card.

4 Use the guillotine to cut each of the rectangles exactly in half. Using double-sided tape, mount the left-hand side of the landscape on one of the smaller pieces of copper card, then on yellow card, then on the larger copper card, making sure each time that the right side has no border, as shown. Carefully secure the piece to the front of the card, aligning the right-most edge of the piece to the right-most edge of the right-hand gatefold.

5 Repeat with the right-hand side of the landscape, this time making sure that the left side has no border. Secure the mounted piece to the left-hand gatefold, aligning the left-most edge of the piece to the left-most edge of the gatefold.

6 Open up the card and use double-sided tape to attach an 11 x 18.5cm (4¼ x 7¼in) rectangle of copper card to the centre. Mount a 10.5 x 18cm (4¼ x 7in) piece of yellow card on top in the centre.

7 Simply shut the card to finish!

Bourbon Nuts

225g (8oz) Demerara sugar, 175ml (6fl. oz or 5¾USfl. oz) bourbon whiskey, 450g (1lb) whole mixed nuts, 50g (1¾oz) butter, water.

Put the bourbon and sugar into a pan and bring it to the boil. Simmer for three minutes and then remove from heat and add mixed nuts. Stir well until the sugar turns white and grainy, then return the saucepan to the heat and add a few drops of water. Melt the sugar again.

Watching carefully to make sure that the sugar does not burn, cook it for two minutes or until the syrup has turned a caramel colour. Remove the pan from the heat and stir in the butter. Turn the nuts out on to a greased baking sheet and spread them out so each one is separate. Leave to cool – these can be kept in an airtight container for up to two weeks.

Makes about 450g (1lb).

wild west

This wonderful American sunset is such an uplifting, attractive scene – ideal for
Father's Day or a birthday. Alternatively, you could use old photographs or a family
picture and use the same techniques as for the gatefold card.

Childhood Memories

Lovely vintage childhood pictures on this star card – a lovely idea for a father!

Here you can see the inside of the Fisherman's Friend card – a pop-out with a copper mirror porthole. Instructions on how to make pop-outs are on page 122–126.

Fisherman's Friend

This would be a great card for a fishing or boating enthusiast – the copper mirror card is very effective.

American Gold Rush

More Americana and a little tip: one unusual way to make gold nuggets or flakes to add to a card is to take breakfast cereal and paint it gold!

Native American Chief

A final American-themed card, this one uses three different sizes of the same picture against a lovely backing paper that co-ordinates perfectly.

Clearly Yours
This romantic Victorian heart shape makes a very simple but unusual Valentine.

St Valentine's Day
Clearly Yours

I love the effect achieved when you use a sheet of heavyweight acetate for the base of the card – it is pretty and different and as constant cardmakers, that's something we are always searching for!

Perfect for your sweetheart

Materials

One 30 x 21cm (12 x 8¼in) sheet of hearts

One 21 x 15cm (8¼ x 6in) sheet of heavyweight acetate

Gold corner peel-offs

Gold line peel-offs

Scoring board

Embossing stylus

Scissors

Tweezers

Soft cloth

Double-sided sticky tape

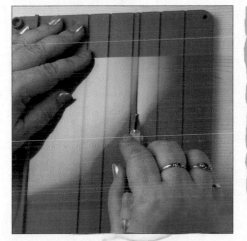

Tip

I have used an embossing stylus rather than a bone folder to score the acetate. This is because the embossing stylus gives a finer, more accurate line which is important when folding acetate.

1 Use the scoring board and embossing stylus to make a crease in the sheet of acetate, then fold it in half.

2 Position the line peel-offs on the front of the acetate, and then overlay the corner peel-offs.

Tip

If the peel-offs you are using do not suit being overlaid, simply trim the line peel-offs with a pair of scissors so that they just touch the corners.

3 Cut out two of the hearts and hold them back-to-back (see inset), and use scissors to make sure that they are both the same size so that no white parts are showing.

4 Use double-sided tape to attach one of the cards to the front of the acetate.

Making a Lavender Sachet

To make fast but beautiful lavender sachets, take a lace-edged handkerchief (well-laundered vintage ones are often particularly stunning). Lay it flat and place a large spoonful of dried lavender or pot pourri in the centre. Gather all four corners together, then the edges, and slip an elastic band round them to secure the sachet into a ball.

Decorate the sachet with pretty satin or organza ribbons and a few miniature silk or paper flowers. This can be hung in a wardrobe or placed with lingerie in a drawer or you can make several and have a pretty bowl of these displayed in the bathroom.

5 Still using double-sided tape, secure the second heart to the inside front of the acetate, covering the white back of the first heart.

6 Take a soft cloth and gently polish the card to remove any fingerprints.

Twisted Vine Heart

The twisted heart is stamped and coloured on acetate, which is then placed over a picture of a single red rose, a lovely and unusual treatment for a Valentine card.

Rose Child

The little girl design is printed out and then embellished with pressed flowers. The card is then covered with a square of acetate held in place with brads to protect the flowers.

Waterfall Hearts

A waterfall mechanism (see pages 50–55 for the technique) is given a twist by using heart-shaped pieces to complete the design – very romantic!

Fans and Flowers

This envelope style card is embellished with embossed parchment fans and some pretty heart-shaped brads.

Only a Rose
Rewarding to create, the waterfall technique is worth reserving for those really special occasions.

Wedding
Only a Rose

This is a wedding card that shows you have taken a lot of time and effort to show how much you care. It incorporates a stylish waterfall effect and is sure to please the happy couple.

Materials

Three 30 x 21cm (12 x 8¼in) sheets of dark green card

One 30 x 21cm (12 x 8¼in) sheet of pale green card

Two 30 x 21cm (12 x 8¼in) sheets of copper mirror card

Rose images

Sheet of backing paper with strip of roses

Green tassel

Green and pale pink ribbons

Three paper roses and two leaves

Two topaz-style brads

Copper line peel-offs

Tweezers

Scissors

Guillotine

Bone folder and scoring board

Japanese screw punch

Cutting board

Double-sided sticky tape

Silicone glue

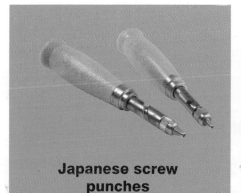

Japanese screw punches

This gadget was originally used in bookbinding and is now widely available for crafters to use for many other purposes – it has a ratchet action so it gracefully slides through several layers of card to make holes anywhere on the card.

Tip

You could use a spare strip of decorative paper instead of the strip of roses.

1 Cut the strip of roses from the backing paper, then layer it on to a slightly wider piece of copper card, attaching it with double-sided tape. Repeat the process, layering the copper on to a slightly wider piece of pale green card. Still using double sided tape, stick the assembled piece on to the right-hand end of one of the sheets of dark green card.

Flower Confetti

To make homemade confetti, pick roses from the garden or buy them from a local shop and remove all the petals. Lay them out on a baking tray and leave in a sunny spot. The time they take to dry will vary depending on the temperature and humidity.

Once they are dry take care to put them in an airtight container. I usually avoid white or other very pale roses as they can go somewhat brown and spoil the look of the confetti.

2 Use the guillotine to cut the second sheet of dark green card down so that you can see the strip of roses when the left-hand ends of the pieces of green card are put together, as shown.

3 Use the guillotine to cut down the pale green card so that it is slightly smaller than the dark green card, and use double-sided sticky tape to attach it, leaving a border round the edge. Repeat this with the copper mirror card, and then the rose backing paper. This is your background.

4 Layer up the main picture on to dark green card and then on to copper card in the same way. Put it to one side (see inset), then cut out three square rose pictures and layer them on to copper card. These will form the waterfall.

5 Cut a 6.5 x 30cm (2½ x 11¾in) strip of pale green card. Use a bone folder and ruler to score across the strip at 7cm (2¾in) from the top, then 9.5cm (3¾in) from the top, and again at 12cm (4¾in) from the top.

6 Add a strip of double-sided tape to each of the tops of the three assembled rose pictures. Fold the strip over at the 12cm (4¾in) mark, and attach the first rose picture at the 7cm (2¾in) crease as shown in the inset. Attach the next one at 9.5cm (3¾in), and the final one on the 12cm (4¾in) crease.

7 Cut an 8 x 2cm (3⅛ x ¾in) strip of copper mirror card and attach it to the pale green card just underneath the bottom picture, using double-sided tape.

8 Trim the pale green card to length, then secure the piece to the right-hand side of the background you assembled in step 3 (make sure that you leave enough space for the large rose picture!), using brads through the copper card. You will need to make holes in the copper card and the background piece.

Tip

I used a Japanese screw punch to make the holes in the copper card, but you could use a hole punch, a bradawl or any other tool that makes holes.

9 Punch a hole into the end of the pale green strip and loop the tassel through. Decorate the area with copper peel-off stickers as shown.

10 Use double-sided tape to secure the large rose picture on the left of the waterfall. This completes the front piece.

11 Attach the two pieces by laying the front on top of the back and punching two holes through both. Use both organza ribbons as one to secure the card together, and finish off with a decorative bow before trimming any excess.

Tip

You could also add a pale-coloured sheet of plain paper on the inside to make it easier to write your message.

12 To finish the card, use touches of silicone glue to decorate the copper strip with some paper flowers.

Golden Bride

The bride has been stamped on acetate and then gold leaf applied to make this fabulous card – ideal for a golden wedding!

Bridal Blossoms

An arch-shaped aperture card contains a stamped bride surrounded with clouds of butterflies and pretty blossoms.

Beautiful Bridesmaids

This is another Kate Greenaway illustration that has been decoupaged and displayed behind an acrylic dome – such a pretty effect.

wedding wishes

This uses the envelope design you can find on page 34 – this looks so pretty and festive, ideal for a spring or summer wedding!

Anniversary
High Spirits

T his light-hearted card makes a lovely anniversary card and the lace and pearl embellishments add that romantic touch to complete the effect!

Materials

Two 30 x 21cm (12 x 8¼in)
sheets of duck-egg blue card
One 30 x 21cm (12 x 8¼in)
sheet of antique gold card
One 30 x 21cm (12 x 8¼in)
sheet of off-white card
Three identical Victorian-style
photographs of a courting couple
Paper lace ribbons
Self-adhesive pearls
15mm (½in) bronze ribbon
7mm (¼in) pale blue ribbon
Tweezers
Double-sided tape
Foam tape
Guillotine
Scissors
Bone folder and scoring board
Silicone glue

1 Keep one of the pictures intact. Cut the lady and gentleman out of the second, and cut out just the upper body of the lady and her parasol from the third.

2 Attach the intact picture to off-white card with double-sided tape, then trim, leaving a 5mm (⅛in) border all round. Repeat the process with duck-egg blue card, again allowing for a 5mm (⅛in) border.

High Spirits

This fun decoupaged card is perfect for any anniversary
– whether it is a first or sixty-first!

3 Fold the sheet of duck-egg blue card in half and use a bone folder to sharpen the crease.

4 Cut a piece of gold card to 14 × 20cm (5½ × 7⅞in), then peel the backing from the lace ribbon and stick a strip down one of the long sides. Tuck the ends of the ribbon behind the card, then attach a second strip across the bottom, tidily tucking the ends behind as before.

5 Attach the gold card to the folded blue card, using 2mm (1/32in) foam tape; then attach the mounted picture on top of the gold card, again using 2mm (1/32in) foam tape.

6 Apply the pearl strips along the lace ribbon. You may need to apply a few single pearls to ensure a neat finish.

7 Tie the bronze and blue ribbons along the spine of the card, making sure that the bow ends up where there is most space in the centre of the photograph. Treat both as a single ribbon to make it easier for yourself.

8 Give the second picture (lady and gentleman) a gentle curve with your fingers and attach it to the card with silicone glue (see inset).

9 Curve and secure the top piece in the same way to finish the card. Remember to allow the card to dry overnight before putting it in an envelope.

A list of the Main Anniversaries

Year	Traditional gift	Modern gift
1	Paper	Clock
2	Cotton	China
3	Leather	Crystal
4	Linen	Fruit and flowers
5	Wood	Silverware
6	Iron	Sugar
7	Copper	Desk set
8	Bronze	Bronze
9	Willow	Linen
10	Tin	Leather
11	Steel	Jewellery
12	Silk	Pearls
13	Lace	Textiles
14	Ivory	Gold jewellery
15	Crystal	Wristwatch
20	China	Platinum
25	Silver	Silver
30	Pearl	Diamond
35	Coral	Jade
40	Ruby	Ruby
45	Sapphire	Sapphire
50	Gold	Gold
55	Emerald	Emerald
60	Diamond	Diamond
65	Blue sapphire	Blue sapphire
70	Platinum	Platinum

This is the centre of the Dancing with Shadows card, which uses the method shown on pages 122–126 to make a pop-out, with the oval pop-out changed to a rectangle.

Clockwise from left:

Heartfelt Greetings

The hearts are stamped and embossed with gold embossing powder, then cut out to make this elegant and sophisticated anniversary card.

Gatefold Silhouettes

Identical images have been paired here to make the cover of the card and then a silver-embossed Victorian doily image has been stamped inside the card.

Dancing with Shadows

This card has a lovely centre (see the inset) and the cover is decorated with miniature flowers and a simple topper.

Anniversary Ribbons

This card has a lovely unusual fold that can be used for lots of different themes.

Thank you
Leopard Song

This jungle cat design is drawn by Jayne Netley Mayhew and is magnificent. All the big cats are beautiful subjects for artists, and here the atmosphere has been captured so well. The card is so very simple but it works brilliantly and you will find it a very useful design to repeat with other images and ideas.

Materials

One 30 x 21cm (12 x 8¼in) sheet of antique gold card

Two 30 x 21cm (12 x 8¼in) sheets of black card

One 30 x 21cm (12 x 8¼in) sheet of hieroglyphic backing card

Two different African-themed backing papers and a large leopard picture

Double-sided tape

Tweezers

Scissors

Guillotine

2mm (¹⁄₃₂in) foam tape

Bone folder and scoring board

1 Fold one of the sheets of black card in half and sharpen the crease with a bone folder. Open it out and cut the front from corner to corner as shown, using a guillotine or paper trimmer. Put the triangle this makes to one side.

Tip

Simple, multi-purpose cards like this one can be made in advance and kept handily stored together with a stamped envelope, so that when you need a thank you card, all you have to do is add your message and address the envelope – much easier and you are more likely to get your thank yous out promptly!

2 Cut the antique gold card down until it fits within the inside of the card, with a 5mm (⅛in) border all round. Mount this on the inside of the card with double-sided tape, then repeat the process with the backing paper, again leaving a 5mm (⅛in) border.

3 Using the extra triangle of card as a guide, cut a slightly smaller triangle from the second style of backing paper and secure it to the flap of the card using double-sided tape.

4 Cut out the largest leopard picture and mount it on a slightly larger piece of black card with double-sided tape. Mount this on a piece of gold card that it slightly larger again.

5 Using the double-sided tape on the left-hand side of the leopard picture, attach it to the card so that it overlaps the cut-away triangle.

Leopard Song

This is a favourite card of mine, as it is simple but effective – and I love big cats! The two complementary backing papers sit so well with this picture.

Opposite from top:

Bouquet of Blues

Pressed flowers take centre stage on this card and the pretty metallic corners are peel-offs.

Blue Carnations

This is one of my favourite cards. The fans are embossed in peacock blue on parchment and teamed with blue carnations and a matching backing paper.

Musical Flowers

Musical backing sheets are useful as a nice neutral base – so many other things match well with them. Here we have flowers and music together: ideal as a thank you for a lovely night out!

Opulent Embossing

The same stamp has been embossed in an antique gold several times for this card and the centre of the stamp has been layered to add a little depth to the card.

Passion Flowers

I love passion flowers, I have them growing all round my studios and here they are teamed with embossed stamping on parchment.

Congratulations
Life at Sea

Old family photographs, or vintage photographs that you have collected, can be used very effectively in making cards – here the same young man is pictured as a boy and then an adult, and the photographs are used together as an exam congratulations card.

Materials

Two 30 x 21cm (12 x 8¼in) sheets of gold mirror card

One 21 x 15cm (8¼ x 6in) sheet of William Morris design backing paper

One 42 x 30cm (16½ x 12in) sheet of dark brown card

Suitable photographs

Embellishments (in this case two buttons and a key)

Double-sided sticky tape

Guillotine

Silicone glue and cocktail stick

1 Fold the brown card in half and sharpen the crease with a bone folder. Use a guillotine to cut the card down to 21 x 16.5cm (8¼ x 6½in).

2 Cut a 20 x 15.5cm (7⅞ x 6⅛in) piece of gold card; and a 19 x 14.5cm (7½ x 5¾in) piece of William Morris backing paper. Mount the backing paper on the gold card with double-sided tape.

3 Attach 2mm (¹⁄₃₂in) foam tape to the back of the gold card, then peel off the backing and attach it to the front of the card.

Remember, people will judge you by your actions, not your intentions. You may have a heart of gold – but so does a hard-boiled egg.

Anonymous

4 Mount the main photograph on gold card, as in step 2, leaving a 5mm (⅛in) border of gold showing, then attach it to the front of the card with double-sided sticky tape.

5 Use the guillotine to crop the smaller photograph so that it fits well in the remaining space (see inset), then mount it on gold card and secure it to the front of the card with double-sided tape.

6 Embellish the card with the key and buttons, securing them with silicone glue.

Life at Sea

This is a gentle vintage card to celebrate someone's success!

Da Vinci Card

These drawings by Leonardo da Vinci make an excellent masculine background for an exam congratulations card.

Vintage Seal

A collection of lovely vintage bits and pieces are used here, with a faux wax seal, a stamped book and sepia photo – ideal for an older person's success maybe?

Clockwise from top left:

School's Out!

A graduation congratulations card here, made
using die-cuts and a rosette.

Coming Through!

A fun card celebrating someone passing their
driving test. I think the torn 'L' plate looks
particularly effective!

Outstanding Success

This wonderful exploding box (see pages 88–91
for the technique) is themed for exam success,
even down to the mortar board shaped top.

Infant Treasures

This is a lovely card to make for a new baby. It incorporates
stamping techniques and a fun shaker feature.

Materials

Two 30 x 21cm (12 x 8¼in)
sheets of pale lilac card

One 30 x 21cm (12 x 8¼in)
sheet of pale blue card

One 30 x 21cm (12 x 8¼in)
sheet of pearl white card

One 21 x 15cm (8¼ x 6in)
sheet of heavyweight acetate

One 21 x 15cm (8¼ x 6in)
sheet of baby-themed backing paper

Pack of coloured small safety pins

Pale blue and lilac organza ribbon

3.5cm (1½in) square craft punch

Rubber stamp: vintage baby

Dark blue archival inkpad

Scissors

2mm (¹⁄₃₂in) foam tape

Tweezers

Double-sided tape

Bone folder and scoring board

Silicone glue

Christening
Infant Treasures

Shaker box features are fun to include in a card. Once you have learnt the technique explained here, you could use little die-cut crystals to look like snow, small beads or a multitude of other things that are small enough to shake and make an attractive addition to the card!

A great card to mark a baby's naming

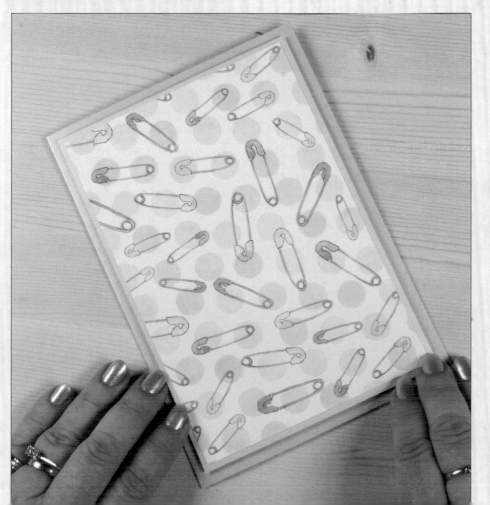

I Score one of the sheets of lilac card down the centre and fold it in half. Sharpen the crease with the bone folder. Trim the pale blue card down until it fits on the front of the folded card, leaving a 5mm (⅛in) border all the way round. Cut the baby-themed backing paper down until it leaves a 5mm (⅛in) border all the way round when laid on the blue piece. Secure it to the blue piece with double-sided tape, and then use 2mm (¹⁄₃₂in) foam tape to secure the completed piece to the card.

To the world you may be one person, but to one person you may be the world.

Anonymous

Babies and Lace

The attractive corners are made by using a corner punch and the lace peeping through from behind the topper is a small paper lace doily.

Before you were conceived, I wanted you.

Before you were born, I loved you.

Before you were here an hour, I would die for you.

This is the miracle of love.

Maureen Hawkins

76

Me and my Rabbit
A lovely gentle watercolour card that uses stamping on a lacy background.

Go Rocking Horse!
Rocking horses are favourites from many people's childhoods and this traditional image is a die-cut that has been coloured by hand.

Baby Love
A pretty waterfall card embellished with lace, pearls and a tassel; perfect for a baby girl.

Christmas
Holy Night

Christmas is one of my favourite times of year and this card says it all. The glittery snow sums up a white Christmas beautifully for me!

Materials

One 30 x 21cm (12 x 8¼in) church scene picture

One 30 x 21cm (12 x 8¼in) sheet of red pearly card

One 30 x 21cm (12 x 8¼in) sheet of antique gold card

One 42 x 30cm (16½ x 12in) sheet of white pearl card

Snowy glitter

15mm (½in) burgundy ribbon

7mm (¼in) gold ribbon

Small adhesive craft jewels

Glue pen

2mm (¹⁄₃₂in) foam tape

Double-sided tape

Guillotine

Bone folder

Scissors

Glue pen

There are several brands of glue pen, but all are basically just that: glue in a pen. It appears blue but then dries clear. As it is in a pen, it is easy to apply, even to smaller areas of your card – I think this is a must-have tool!!

Holy Night

A lovely picture of an old English church, made even prettier by adding some glue and snowy glitter liberally at the end.

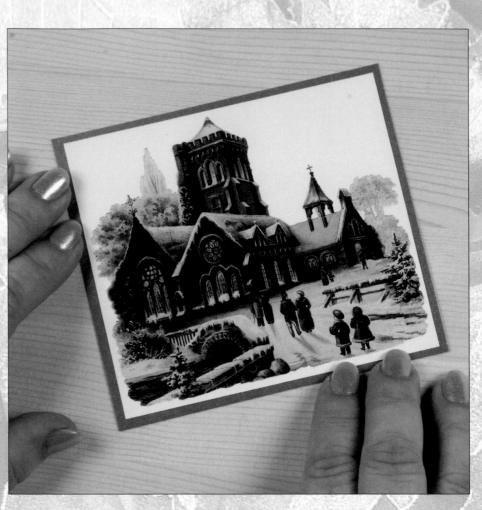

1 Fold the white card in half, sharpen the crease with a bone folder and trim to 18 × 21cm (7 × 8¼in) using a guillotine.

2 Cut out the largest church scene, and make a gold mount for it that is 5mm (¼in) larger all round. Secure the scene to the front of the mount with double-sided tape.

3 Make a red mount for the piece that is 10mm (½in) larger than the gold mount; then make a second gold mount 5mm (¼in) larger than the red mount. Secure the piece to the red mount with 2mm (⅛in) foam tape; then attach it all to the second gold mount using double-sided tape.

4 Place foam tape on the back of the larger gold mount, remove the backing and place on the front of the card.

5 Open up the card and place the two ribbons against the spine, using them as one (see inset). Close the card and tie a bow to hold the ribbon in place. Trim away any excess ribbon using the scissors.

6 Use the glue pen to scribble over the snowy areas on the picture.

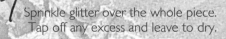

7 Sprinkle glitter over the whole piece. Tap off any excess and leave to dry.

7 Finish the card by attaching craft jewels along the ribbon.

Mulled wine – Victoria Farm style

75cl (1 bottle) claret or other red wine
150ml (¼pt) unsweetened orange juice
150ml (¼pt) water
150ml (¼pt) port
50g (1¾oz) Demerara or brown sugar
7g (1 heaped tsp) mixed spice
2 large juicy oranges each cut into eight pieces
8 cinnamon sticks

Put all the ingredients, except the cinnamon sticks, in a saucepan and place on a very low heat. Gently warm the mull for an hour or so.

If you want to prepare it in advance, warm it for an hour, leave to cool and then reheat when needed.

Serve in very tough glasses or mugs with the cinnamon sticks as stirrers. Do not include any of the pieces of orange in the glasses as they have an embarrassing habit of falling on your nose as you try and drink.

Serves eight non-drivers!

Adapting Commercial Christmas Crackers

If you go shopping for crackers and find some completely plain gold or silver crackers – get the least patterned outsides you can – then you can decorate them with a stamped and glittered image, some organza ribbon or some pearls or small silk flowers.

Try focusing on the contents, too – putting your own charms inside can be more interesting, and will certainly be more personal.

You will end up with unique crackers that are far prettier and more fun than choosing the ones in the shops that have nothing but plastic inside!

From left to right:

The Snow Family

This lovely stamped and coloured card features a snowman couple. The smaller image below is done on shrink plastic (see pages 116–119 for the technique).

Christmas Angel

This angelic little girl is one of my favourite Christmas-themed images. You can make this card using the same directions as for Leopard Song (see pages 64–65). This keeps it fairly simple in case you are sending out a few!

Christmas Cooking!

Another of my favourite vintage Christmas images with an enthusiastic little girl baking Christmas cookies – so sweet!

Christmas
Santa Box

The is a simple set of instructions to make an exploding box – which you can then embellish as intricately or simply as you wish.

Craft punches

Craft punches come in various shapes and sizes – in this project I have used a corner punch that quickly nips the corner into an attractive shape. But you can also find border or edge punches that decorate the sides of your card or standard shape punches that are available in everything from a giraffe to a geometric shape.

Materials

Two 30 x 21cm (12 x 8¼in) sheets of cream card

One 21 x 15cm (8¼ x 6in) sheet of red plaid paper

One 21 x 15cm (8¼ x 6in) sheet of green plaid paper

One 30 x 21cm (12 x 8¼in) sheet of gold mirror card

Four sheets of star-shaped Santa embellishments

Small red poinsettia paper flower

Soft pencil and eraser

2mm (1/32in) foam tape

Scissors

Tweezers

Double-sided tape

Ruler and embossing stylus

Decorative corner craft punch

Silicone glue and cocktail stick

Santa Box
You could put a little treat in the middle of the box – perhaps a mini mince pie for Santa?

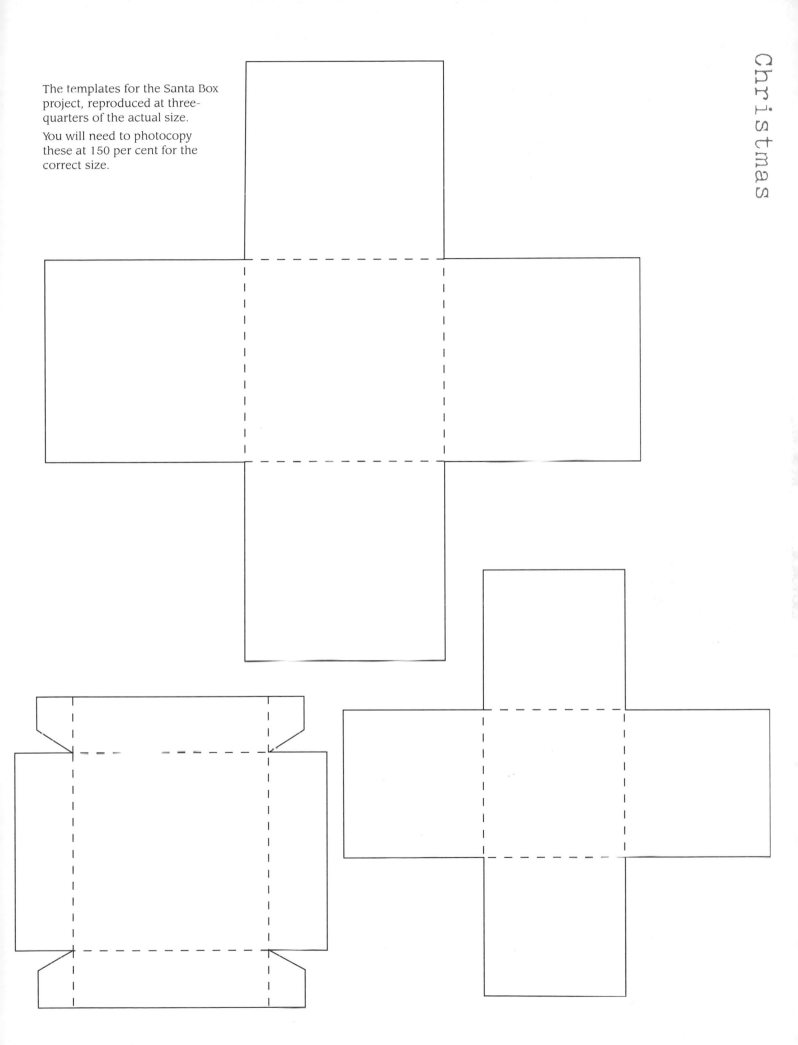

The templates for the Santa Box project, reproduced at three-quarters of the actual size.

You will need to photocopy these at 150 per cent for the correct size.

1 Using a soft pencil, trace round the three pieces of the template on to cream card, then cut them out carefully.

2 Using the embossing stylus and ruler, score between each tab on the lid, as shown.

3 Score from the inside point across each side of the cross, then repeat on the smaller cross-shaped piece.

4 Use the decorative corner punch to punch all of the corners of the two other pieces.

Tip

I always use craft punches upside down, so that I can make sure that the punch is in exactly the right place.

5 Take the red plaid paper and cut out four 6cm (2½in) squares. Use double-sided tape to attach one to each of the inner faces of the large cross. Use the punched corners as a guide to fitting the paper in the right place.

6 Cut four 4cm (1½in) squares from the green plaid paper and attach them to the inner faces of the smaller cross. Again, you can use the punched corners to make sure the squares are in the right place.

7 Add small pieces of double-sided tape to the outside of the tabs on the lid, remove the backing, and then fold them inside the edges to make the lid.

8 Cut five 6cm (2½cm) squares of gold card, five 5.5cm (2in) squares of red plaid paper, and five 4cm (1½in) squares of green plaid paper. Mount a green square on each of the red squares, and then mount the red squares on the gold squares, securing them with double-sided tape. Use double-sided tape to fix four of the assembled pieces to the outside of the large cross.

9 Fix the last piece on to the top of the lid, again using double-sided tape. Embellish it with the paper poinsettia, fixing it with silicone glue.

10 Cut out eight of the smallest star-shaped Santa embellishments, two of each design, and attach four to the outside of the large cross, and four to the inside of the small cross as shown, using 2mm (¹⁄₃₂in) foam tape.

11 Cut a 4cm (1½in) square from gold card, and attach it to the centre of the small cross with double-sided tape. Tape the small cross to the centre of the large cross.

12 Fold the sides of both boxes up, and put the lid on top to finish.

Christmas Celebration

This card combines the pop-out instructions and the star card idea – very effective and not too difficult if you take it stage by stage.

Madonna and Child

This pretty traditional stamp looks wonderful and makes the card very easy to do, which means it lends itself to multiple Christmas card production!

christmas window

This landscape card is a very simple use of two images, one smaller than the other, which works very effectively.

Snowman Shaker card

The snowmen on this shaker card (see pages 72–75 for the technique) are behind a sheet of acetate. The space can be filled with small sparkly beads or crystals, fake snow or whatever you have handy that would pass for a snowstorm!

With sympathy
Remembered

This is a fabulous image for a sympathy card – and adding the embossed parchment embellishments makes it very special. It is not possible to know when you might need a sympathy card, but you can always keep some half-made in a safe place to complete should the need arise, or just play with stamping on parchment and keep the pieces in a handy drawer.

Materials

One 42 x 30cm (16½ x 12in) sheet of pale lilac card

One 30 x 21cm (12 x 8¼in) sheet of dark blue card

One 30 x 21cm (12 x 8¼in) sheet of lily pictures

One 30 x 21cm (12 x 8¼in) sheet of lily backing paper

One 30 x 21cm (12 x 8¼in) sheet of 140gsm parchment

One 21 x 15cm (8¼ x 6in) sheet of acetate

Gold and silver butterfly peel-offs

Two Victorian doily-style stamps: heart and oval

Embossing pad

White embossing powder

Tweezers

Guillotine

Bone folder

Scissors

Heat tool

Silicone glue and cocktail stick

Acrylic block

Double-sided tape

Embossing powder, embossing pad and heat tool

Embossing powders are available in an enormous range of colours and textures and are my preferred method of embossing. I use one embossing pad and have lots of different colours of powder to play with.

Try and choose a detail powder for finer work as these allow more of the stamp's detail to remain. There are also glittery powders, textured powders and extra thick powders – try experimenting with them all!

There are also several varieties of heat tool available – they tend to work on very similar principles so I would simply suggest investing in a good make and I am sure it will be fine!

1 Trim the dark blue card to 18cm (7in) square. Fold the lilac card in half and cut it down to 21cm (8¼in) square. Use the bone folder to sharpen the crease.

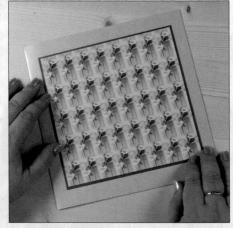

2 Cut the backing paper to 17cm (6¾in) square, and mount it on the dark blue card using double-sided tape. Mount the dark blue square on to the front of the lilac card, again using double-sided tape.

94

3 Stamp both doily stamps on to parchment using the embossing pad. Cover both with embossing powder (see inset), pour away the excess and then heat gently from behind with a heat tool. Once they are fully embossed, cover both with an acrylic block to flatten them. Once they are cool, cut out both shapes.

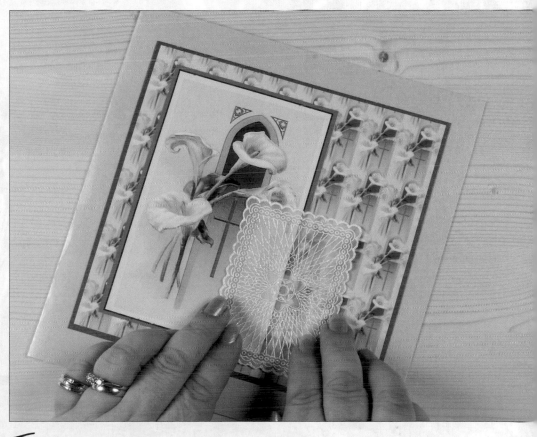

4 Take the peel-off butterflies and put them on to the sheet of acetate. Carefully cut round the butterflies. Doing this gives them real substance and they look much nicer on the card.

5 Cut out and attach a large lily picture to the front of the card with tape, and then use silicone glue to attach the parchment rectangle.

6 Attach the parchment oval on top of the rectangle, and secure a small lily picture on top of the oval; both attached with silicone glue.

7 Secure the butterflies in place with silicone glue to finish the card. Allow it to dry overnight before packaging it up and posting it off.

Remembered

Although this has been designed as a sympathy card it could also be suitable for a wedding if you add a little white or lilac organza ribbon: lilies are wonderful flowers that symbolise so many things!

Do Not Stand at my Grave and Weep

Do not stand at my grave
  and weep
I am not there; I do not sleep.
I am a thousand winds that blow,
I am the diamond glints on snow.
I am the sun on ripened grain,
I am the gentle autumn rain.
When you awaken in the
  morning's hush
I am the swift uplifting rush
Of quiet birds in circled flight.
I am the soft stars that shine
  at night.
Do not stand at my grave
  and cry,
I am not there; I did not die.

Mary Elizabeth Frye – 1932

Victorian Angel

This sympathy card is a basic gatefold shape but has co-ordinating papers on the front of the card as well as inside.

Daffodil Angel

This is another card using the basic fold featured in several of the examples. The corners of the main picture have been rounded with a corner punch.

Sympathy Lilies

This card uses the same image as the main project but here you can see the flowers have been cut out and repeated in the bottom right-hand corner to give a very elegant result.

Missing you
Kitten Curl

The kitten has been stamped on a square piece of acrylic. This makes a fabulous addition to a card as it adds shine, texture and interest all in one. Note that you need to make sure you are using a permanent archival inkpad that is recommended for shiny surfaces to stamp on the acrylic!

Things turn out best for people who make the best of the way things turn out.

Anonymous

Squirrel Cake

100g (4oz) margarine
100g (4oz) sugar
100g (4oz) self-raising flour
2 large eggs, beaten
15ml (1tbsp) cold water
10g (2tsp) instant coffee granules (not powder)

Squirrel's Cream

425ml (¾ pint) double cream
45ml (3tbsp) coffee liqueur
45g (3tbsp) chopped hazelnuts, plus extra for decoration

Grease and line two 17.5cm (7in) sponge tins. Cream together the margarine and the sugar until white and creamy. Add the beaten eggs a little at a time and beat well. Using a metal spoon, fold in the sifted flour and add the cold water until a soft consistency is reached.

At the very last moment fold in the instant coffee granules.

Spoon the mixture into the two sandwich tins and spread evenly with a palette knife. Bake in a pre-heated oven at 190°C (375°F) Gas Mark 5 for about twenty minutes. Remove from the oven when they are cooked and turn out on to a wire rack to cool.

When cool, sandwich the two cakes together with the Squirrel's Cream.

Whip the cream and add a little sugar if you wish. Fold in the coffee liqueur and the hazelnuts, and sprinkle the top with extra hazelnuts for decoration.

Archival inkpads, rubber stamps and the acrylic block

When you are stamping, use a permanent archival inkpad, as these are the best for fine detail. This also allows you to use watercolour paint and glue over it without smudging the piece.

All the stamps I have used throughout the book are unmounted rubber. These are also much easier to use than the traditional wood-mounted stamps.

You can get acrylic pieces in all shapes and sizes and it is great fun to play around with, as well as saving you space!

Tip
To achieve a good random effect, it helps to rotate the stamp a little each time you use it.

1 Score down the middle of the off-white card and fold it in half. Trim it down to 15cm (6in) square.

2 Place the main card on to a sheet of scrap paper and stamp the first cat across the edges repeatedly.

3 Cut an 8cm (3⅛in) square of off-white card, and use double-sided tape to mount it on to a 9cm (3½in) square of copper mirror card (see inset). Mount this piece on to the front of the card with 2mm (1/32in) foam tape.

4 Peel off the backing paper from both sides of the acrylic (see inset), and stamp the second cat in the centre using the permanent archival ink.

5 Once the ink is dry, put the acrylic on scrap paper. Use the glue pen to colour the cat quickly and thoroughly and sprinkle copper glitter over it.

Tip

Do not worry about excess glitter at this point. Wait until the glue is completely dry, and then use a large soft brush to gently clean both sides of the acrylic. This can take a little patience, as the glitter can settle on the other side of the acrylic; so do persevere for a good result.

6 Tap off the excess glitter and leave the piece to dry.

7 Use the large-nibbed gold pen to colour the edges of the acrylic.

8 Use a cocktail stick to apply blobs of silicone glue to the back of the acrylic. Make sure that you apply glue only to the glittered area, so that you can not see the glue once the piece is in place. Use double-sided tape to attach the piece to the centre of the card to finish.

Kitten Curl

I love the combination of the glitter on the little cat with the copper mirror card
and the monochrome stamping – fabulous!

Flora the Labrador

A Victorian photomount over lovely art nouveau style papers. This photograph of a much-loved dog was made into a card given to the surprised but appreciative owner.

Envelope Blues

The envelope style that you will have spotted several times within this book comes into its own again here; the lace edging makes a wonderful contrast to the dark blue.

Puppy Pyramage

Here a picture of a puppy has been decoupaged using the technique explained on pages 16–19.

Belated
Butterflies

This card is a fairly complex one as I felt it was nice to send a really special card as an apology for forgetting someone's birthday! It is also a very rewarding piece to make.

The technique used here, of clear embossing across a small image, is a very handy one. Although I have used a slightly sparkly clear crystal, you could use standard clear embossing powder and build up several layers, which also looks effective.

Butterflies
A great card for a birthday, whether it is sent on time or not!

Materials

Two 30 x 21cm (12 x 8¼in) sheets of raspberry card
One 30 x 21cm (12 x 8¼in) sheet of lilac card
Bookmark and sheets of apple blossom design
Three large and two small pearl brads
Ivory-coloured tassel
Butterfly stickers
Glisten embossing powder
Double-sided sticky tape
Embossing pad
Guillotine
Japanese screw punch
Tweezers
Heat tool
Silicone glue and cocktail stick
2mm (¹⁄₃₂in) foam tape

1 Trim approximately 3cm (1¼in) from one of the short ends of the raspberry card, and put the strip safely to one side. Trim the lilac card down to 14.5cm (5¾in) and place it on top of the larger piece of the raspberry card. Put the strip on top of the lilac piece as shown.

Tip

I judge the spacing of the brads by eye, but you can use a ruler if you prefer. Similarly, you can use a hole punch instead of the screw punch - use whatever tools you have!

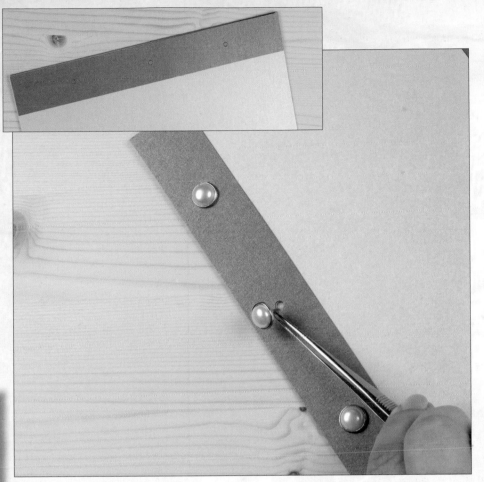

2 Holding the three layers together, make three equally-spaced marks on the strip (see inset), then use the Japanese screw punch to make holes through all three layers. Insert the three brads and fasten the paper by splaying the legs.

Pressed flowers

If you plan to use real pressed flowers on a card why not try the same technique I have used on the paper flowers in this card?

Having glued the pressed flowers down carefully, press the embossing pad across them and sprinkle the clear embossing powder over them (try extra thick embossing powder if you have any).

Heat gently till the crystals melt and then sprinkle more on top. Repeat until you have a clear shimmery glass coating over the flowers – a little like putting them under a glass cover.

3 Cut a small piece of raspberry card approximately 8.5 x 2.5cm (3⅜ x 1in) and place it on the right-hand end of the main card. Attach it by making a hole at either end and securing with the small brads. This piece will secure the bookmark.

4 Cut out the bookmark from the sheet, make a hole at the bottom with the Japanese screw punch and secure the tassel through this hole.

5 Prepare the small apple blossom picture by cutting it out and placing it on scrap paper. Cover it entirely with the embossing pad and sprinkle the embossing powder over it.

6 Heat the powder with the heat tool until it melts. Allow to dry, and repeat two or three more times until a sparkly surface is created. Once it is dry, layer it on to a slightly larger piece of the raspberry card, securing it with double-sided tape.

7 Cut out one of the main apple blossom pictures and tape it to a slightly larger piece of raspberry card. Attach this to the lilac piece of the main card, then cut out a second apple blossom picture. Trim away the background from this piece and give it a slight curve with your fingers (see inset), then mount it on top of the first picture using silicone glue and the cocktail stick.

8 Use 2mm (1/32in) foam tape to mount the small apple blossom piece, placing it so that it overlaps the bottom of the large piece.

10 Place as many additional butterfly stickers as you like to finish the card.

9 Slide the bookmark into place and attach a butterfly sticker to the bookmark holder and on the large piece as shown.

Folded Flowers

This card has simply been scored into three equal sections instead of folding it in half to make the card. The resulting fold is very attractive.

A Very Sorry Bear

Again the bear has been simply stamped but instead of having stamped flowers, here he has some little paper flowers as his peace offering!

Sorry Bear

Who could stay angry for long with this bear looking up at you? A simple card with plain stamping and a little colour added to the flowers.

Retirement
Clover Field

A special card that looks a lot more difficult than it actually is – honestly! Have a try – and if in doubt use less water and less paint: you can always add more colour, but it is hard to take it away.

Watercolour crayons and brush

I have used some watercolour crayons for this project but you could use pencils, blocks of paint, or whatever you have in the cupboard.

The brushes you use need to be ones that will behave nicely – cheap, poor quality brushes can cause you a great deal of extra work as they will not hold a good shape and will make splodges all over your work!

Materials

One 42 x 30cm (16½ x 12in) sheet of charcoal grey pearl card

One 30 x 21cm (12 x 8¼in) sheet of royal blue pearl card

One 30 x 21cm (12 x 8¼in) sheet of white card

Two 30 x 21cm (12 x 8¼in) sheets of watercolour paper

Butterfly stickers

Four different botanical flower rubber stamps

Archival black inkpad

Double-sided tape

Tweezers

Guillotine

Bone folder and scoring board

Watercolour crayons and good quality fine brush

Acrylic block

2mm (1/32in) foam tape

1 Score and fold the charcoal grey pearl card in half, sharpening the crease with a bone folder. Use the guillotine to trim the card down to 21cm (8¼in) square. Cut some white paper to 19cm (7½in) square and mount it on the front of the charcoal grey card with double-sided tape.

2 Cut two 8cm (3⅛in) squares and two 8 × 9cm (3⅛ × 3½in) rectangles from the watercolour paper.

Tip

Using a clear acrylic block mount for the stamps makes it easy to see that you are stamping in the right place on the paper.

3 Carefully stamp each of the pieces of watercolour paper with a different botanical stamp.

Don't grumble that roses have thorns: be thankful that thorns have roses.

Tip

I rub the watercolour crayons on to the acrylic block and then take up the colour from there. Do not be too heavy-handed with the colour: you can add more later, but you can not take it away.

4 Colour the four images using the watercolour crayons and brush.

5 Once you have painted the stamped images, put them under another piece of watercolour paper and place a book or similar weight on it so that they dry perfectly flat.

6 Using double-sided tape, mount the squares on to 8.5cm (3¼in) squares of Royal blue card, and the rectangles on to 8.5 x 9.5cm (3¼ x 3¾in) rectangles of royal blue card.

7 Use 2mm (1/32in) foam tape to attach the mounted pieces to the front of the card, and stick some butterfly stickers on as embellishments to finish.

Tip

Why not include some seed packets inside your card?

A garden is a friend you can visit any time.

Clover Field

Four gentle botanical images are paired with some pretty 3D butterflies in this garden-themed retirement card – but it would also make a lovely birthday card too!

A perfect summer day is when the sun is shining, the breeze is blowing, the birds are singing, and the lawn mower is broken.

James Dent

Opposite from top to bottom:

Roses are wild

The background of the card is created by stamping several times with the same wild rose stamp used to create the front. It is then coloured using paints or pens.

Heartfelt wishes

The join on this card is camouflaged by the lacy daisies. The pop-out technique is explained on pages 122–126 but the shape has been changed – in this instance to a heart.

Summer Poppies

This simple but very effective card is created using three identical images and placing them at different heights for a gorgeous result!

New home Moving Day

I love playing with shrink plastic. Once you have got over any initial panic – as it often behaves in an unexpected fashion – then you'll love it too!

Moving Day

A romantic English thatched cottage (mine is a little like this!) and a miniature tea set – no wonder this is one of my favourite cards in this book!

Materials

One 42 x 30cm (16½ x 12in) sheet of white pearl card
One 30 x 21cm (12 x 8¼in) sheet of pale coral card
One 30 x 21cm (12 x 8¼in) sheet of gold card
One sheet of country cottage-themed decoupage,
including a 10.5 x 14.8cm (4⅛ x 5⅞in)
sheet of backing paper
One small white doily
Two sheets of white shrink plastic
Four different afternoon tea stamps
Archival royal blue inkpad
Silicone glue and cocktail stick
Tweezers
Double-sided tape
Bone folder and scoring tool
Guillotine and sharp scissors
Acrylic mounting block
Heat tool

1 Fold the white pearl card in half using the bone folder and scoring tool, then use the guillotine to trim it to 21 × 23cm (8¼ × 9in). Cut a 19 × 21cm (7½ × 8¼in) piece of gold card and use double-sided tape to mount it on top of the card. Cut a 17.5 × 20.5cm (6⅞ × 8in) piece of pale coral card and mount that on top of the gold card.

Pear and Blackberry Pie

675g (1½lb) self-raising flour
450g (1lb) white vegetable fat
6–8 Conference pears
450g (1lb) blackberries
45g (3tbsp) Demerara sugar
Water

Peel, core and then slice the pears. Cook them, together with 30g (2tbsp) of the sugar, in enough water to cover them. It is important to cook them gently to keep their shape. Leave to cool.

Cook the blackberries with a little water and the remaining sugar and then leave them to cool. I feel it is better to leave the pears and blackberries separate – it makes no difference to the taste but it does improve the look of the finished filling.

Make the pastry by rubbing the fat into the flour until it resembles breadcrumbs, then add about a cupful of water to form a soft dough. Divide the dough in half and gently roll out the first half on a very well-floured board. Lift the pastry by folding it over a rolling pin and line a greased 30cm (12in) dish with it.

A straight-sided dish will make the pie easier to serve. Mould the pastry round the edges of the dish and trim off any excess.

Still keeping them apart, drain both the pears and blackberries, saving some of the juice. Cover the base of the pie with the pear slices and then cover them with the blackberries, before spooning the remaining juice over the fruit.

Roll out the other half of the pastry, then moisten the edges of the bottom layer of pastry with water. Place the pastry top over the pie to make a lid. Press gently around the edges and trim off any excess. Brush the top of the pie with milk (or a mixture of milk and egg yolk), then use any scraps of pastry to decorate the top of the pie with leaves, apples or any other design you like.

Bake in a pre-heated oven at 200°C (400°F), Gas Mark 6 for 25–30 minutes or until the pastry is cooked and golden brown.

2 Cut out the main picture and the backing paper from the decoupage sheet, and mount both on gold card. Use the guillotine to trim the gold card down until there is only a 5mm (⅛in) border round each.

3 Stick the mounted backing paper piece to the main card with double-sided tape. Attach the paper doily to the bottom right of the centre of the card using silicone glue.

4 Use the sharp scissors to carefully cut out the decoupage pieces. Give them each a slight curve with your finger.

5 Stick the mounted main picture to the main card as shown, then use silicone glue and a cocktail stick to attach the decoupage pieces in turn. The large house is the first layer, and the flowerbed and three pieces of the thatched roof go on top of that.

6 Press the teapot stamp on to the archival inkpad, then press it on to the shrink plastic.

7 Use the various designs to stamp two plates, one jam pot and three teacups on to the shrink plastic. Use small sharp scissors to cut out each piece, being extremely careful and cutting as close as you can to the lines. Remember to cut out the inside of the teapot and teacup handle, too.

Tip

Never, ever use your heat tool near your craft mat as it will warp it.

Tip

As the plastic shrinks, the colours get darker as the pigments get closer together. Bear this in mind when picking your ink colour, and go for a shade lighter than you would like the finished piece to end up.

8 Hold one of the pieces on a heatproof surface with your tweezers, and use the heat tool to shrink it. It will curl up, but do not lose your nerve! Keep heating it until it flattens back out. Immediately place the large acrylic block on top of it to make sure that it is completely flat (see inset) and turn off your heat tool.

9 Repeat with all of the shrink plastic pieces.

10 Use silicone glue to mount the shrink plastic pieces on to the doily to finish.

119

Silhouette Builders
This new home card has an unusual twist: fairy folk building a little home.

Rose Cottage
Real pressed roses and leaves twist round this unashamedly romantic new home card with more English cottages!

Roses round the Door
A lovely bright red die-cut front door has been made into a shaker card with little blossoms behind the acetate.

An Overseas Home
This card was designed for those making a move overseas. The lady is gazing fondly over the water towards her old home.

New job
Dive Right In

Having a pop-out feature in the centre of your card is fun and adds a little something different – following these instructions it can be very simple.

Materials

One sheet of penguin toppers and two sheets of penguin backing paper

One 30 x 21cm (12 x 8¼in) sheet of gunmetal card

One 30 x 21cm (12 x 8¼in) sheet of white card

Two 30 x 21cm (12 x 8¼in) sheets of very dark green card

Double-sided tape

Guillotine

Bone folder

White pencil

Tweezers

2mm (¹⁄₃₂in) foam tape

Silicone glue and cocktail stick

Opposite:

Dive Right In

The flock of penguins are waving goodbye – well, that's how I saw it! A fun card to say 'good luck in your new job from all of us'.

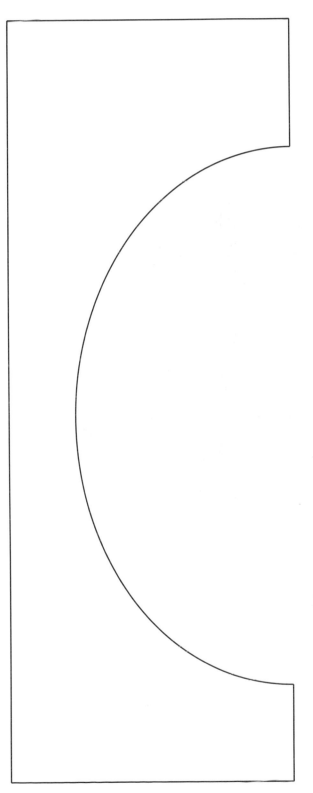

The template for the Dive Right In project, reproduced at actual size.

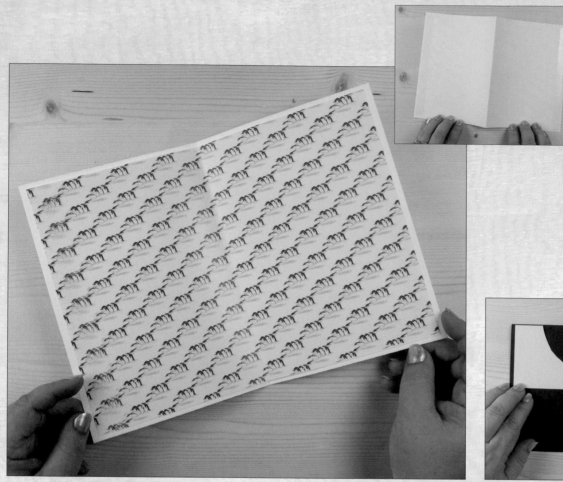

1 Fold the white card in half, then trim the small penguin backing paper to slightly smaller than the inside of the card and fold it in half. Run double-sided tape down the short ends of the back of the backing paper as shown (see inset). Remove the backing and attach it to the inside of the card.

2 Fold one of the sheets of very dark green card in half and place the template on top with the open side of the oval on the fold.

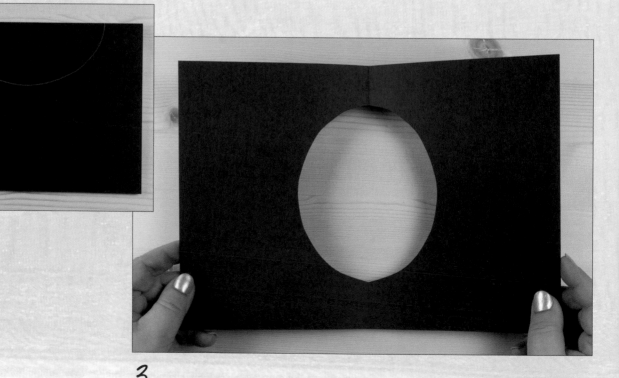

3 Trace round the inside of the oval with a white pencil (see inset), and then use scissors to cut along the white line. This makes an oval hole in the centre of the card when it is opened up.

4 Turn the card over so that the fold is pointing upwards, and make a concertina fold by bending the left-hand edge over to reach the fold. Use a bone folder to sharpen the crease, then repeat on the right-hand side.

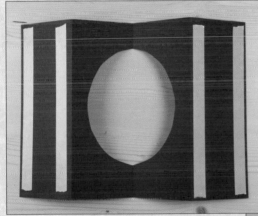

5 Turn the card over so the fold is pointing down, and run double-sided tape down the sides as shown (see inset). Remove the backing and secure to the card, aligning the edge of the black card to the edge of the white card.

6 Use the guillotine to cut a 13 × 19cm (5 × 7½in) piece of very dark green card and use double-sided tape to mount it on a piece of gunmetal card 14 × 20cm (5½ × 7¾in). Cut a piece of the blue water backing paper down to 12 × 18cm (4¾ × 7in), and mount this on the very dark green card.

7 Use 2mm (1/32in) foam tape to mount the piece on the front of the card.

8 Cut out the two largest groups of penguins from the toppers and trim off the diving penguin on the left of each group. Give each group a curve with your fingers and use a large amount of silicone glue to attach them to the front of the card and give a raised feel. Attach the second group slightly below the first to give the impression that there is a really large group of penguins.

9 Smear silicone glue over the diving penguins and attach them to the front to finish the card, using the tweezers to place them carefully.

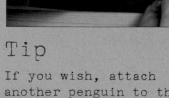

Tip

If you wish, attach another penguin to the inside of the card.

Our Little Fairy
A charming fairy waving goodbye. Paired with marbled papers, it looks lovely.

Lilac Blossom
Individual die-cut flower heads have been assembled to look like a trail of lilac.

Business Tycoons
A great vintage image, ideal for a man moving on from the office!

Hollywood Dreams
This card really captures the hopes we have when we move to pastures new.

Model Behaviour
A pyramage effect card featuring a young lady off to make her fortune!

Index

acetate 10, 12, 28, 30, 32, 39, 47, 49, 56, 73, 74, 93, 94, 95, 121
acrylic 100, 102
acrylic block 94, 95, 100, 110, 111, 112, 116, 119
African 64
Albert Schweitzer 30
American 40, 43, 45
aperture card 56

baby 73, 74
backing paper 11, 17, 23, 25, 36, 45, 51, 64, 66, 73, 94, 116, 117, 123, 124, 126
badge 22
bear 109
bone folder 10, 23, 40, 51, 53, 58, 60, 64, 73, 78, 110, 116, 123
bookmark 14, 106, 108, 109
bougainvillea 14
brads 9, 49, 51, 106, 107
butterfly 14, 39, 56, 94, 95, 106, 109, 110, 113, 114

carnations 66
cat 23, 25, 64, 66, 100, 101, 102, 104
cocktail stick 10, 11, 34, 86, 94, 100, 103, 108, 116, 118, 123
corner punch see craft punch
craft jewels 9, 78, 82
craft punch 20, 39, 73, 74, 76, 86, 89, 99

decoupage 8, 9, 20, 27, 35, 36, 39, 57, 59, 105, 116, 117, 118
design CDs 10, 28, 39
die-cutter 23, 26
die-cutting 14, 23, 26, 70, 73, 77, 121, 127
dog 20, 105
doily 62, 76, 94, 95, 116, 117, 119

Egyptian 17, 18
embellishment 9, 20, 32, 33, 58, 68, 86, 90, 94, 113
embossing 14, 15, 49, 62, 66, 94, 106
embossing pad 94, 95, 106, 107, 108
embossing powder 62, 94, 95, 106, 107, 108
embossing stylus 9, 47, 86, 88
envelope card 34, 36, 49, 57, 105
exploding box 32, 39, 70, 86

face 19
fans 14, 15, 30, 49
felt-tip pens 9, 100, 103
flowers 35, 37, 99, 110
foliage 12

gatefold 21, 27, 41, 43, 98
glitter 78, 81, 100, 102, 104
glue pen 78, 81, 100, 102
gold leaf 28, 32, 56

heat tool 94, 95, 106, 108, 119

ink, archival 9, 28, 30, 73, 74, 100, 102, 110, 118
inkpad 20, 28, 73, 100, 110

James Dent 114
Japanese screw punch 10, 12, 51, 54, 106, 107, 108
Jayne Netley Mayhew 10, 64

Kate Greenaway 27, 39, 57

lace 76, 77, 114
landscape 17, 18, 41, 93
large soft brush 9, 100, 102
Leonardo da Vinci 70
lid 88, 90, 91
lily 94, 96, 97

map 20
Mary Elizabeth Frye 98
Maureen Hawkins 76
mirror card 44, 45, 51, 52, 53, 68, 86, 100, 101, 104

organza 9, 10, 39, 55, 73, 83, 97

paintbrush 9, 110, 112
paper flowers 51, 55, 86, 107, 109, 127
parchment 14, 15, 49, 66, 94, 95
passion flowers 66
peel-off stickers 9, 28, 31, 36, 47, 51, 54, 66, 94, 95
periwinkle 10, 11, 13
photograph 15, 28, 39, 43, 58, 61, 68, 69
pictures 25, 28, 52, 54
pocket 20, 25
poinsettia 90

pop-out 44, 62, 92, 114, 123
preserving roses 12
pressed flowers and leaves 10, 11, 12, 49, 66, 107, 121
printing 32
pyramage 16, 17, 21, 127

rose 12, 15, 50, 51, 52, 53, 54, 114
ribbon 9, 10, 12, 15, 23, 25, 28, 31, 39, 51, 55, 58, 60, 61, 73, 75, 78, 81, 83, 97
rubber stamps 9, 28, 92, 94, 95, 100, 101, 110, 114, 118

safety pins 73, 74, 75
scoring board 10, 23, 40, 47, 51, 58, 64, 73, 110
sepia 20, 28, 70
shaker card 72, 73, 75, 93, 121
shrink plastic 84, 116, 118, 119
silicone glue 10, 11, 12, 19, 28, 31, 34, 35, 36, 51, 55, 61, 69, 75, 86, 90, 94, 95, 96, 100, 103, 106, 108, 116, 117, 118, 119, 123, 126
snowman 84
stamping 15, 32, 56, 62, 66, 70, 72, 73, 77, 84, 95, 102, 104, 109, 111, 114
star card 23, 26, 33, 92
stickers 9, 31, 106, 109, 110, 113

tags 20
tassels 9, 51, 77, 106, 108
templates 87, 88, 123, 124
topper 21, 27, 39, 62, 123
Tutankhamun 17, 19

Victorian 27, 32, 39, 46, 58, 94, 105
vintage 20, 32, 44, 68, 70, 84, 127
voucher 25

watercolour 9, 10, 77, 110, 111, 112
watercolour crayons 110, 112
waterfall 15, 49, 50, 51, 52, 54, 77
William Morris 68